HOW TO GET YOUR SHIT TOGETHER

and start making money

PETER RUECKER

CONTENTS

PART TWO: MAKE MONEY

INTRODUCTION

I want you to get your shit together

I spent many nights in high school and college going to parties, and many days in my early career showing up to work with a raging hangover. At first, this was fun. However, as I started getting older the party scene started getting old too. *Did I want to live my life living for the weekend? How many nightclubs and bars was I going to blow my paycheck on?*

As I began to realize how shallow the party scene was I started asking myself deeper questions: *How was I going to support myself long term? Was I reaching my professional potential if I was showing up hungover each Monday?*

These are the kinds of questions I started asking myself a couple years after college. The longer I was out of school and away from the comforts of home, the more I realized that life is hard.

There wasn't a singular moment that made me want to get my shit together. Instead, my cumulative life experiences and observations about others, motivated me to get serious. I realized I didn't want to keep living this way. I saw how lucky I was to have my family's social network and my ability to connect with people, which kept opportunities open even when I didn't deserve them. I realized I'd better get my shit together.

And you probably do too.

Getting my shit together took a lot of hard work. But in hindsight, I realize how lucky I was. I had support and knowledge passed to me by people who could help. That's why I'm passing it forward. I want you to know that it's totally possible to get your shit together, as long as you're willing to step up and do the work.

Here's how I got my shit together and crafted a successful and fulfilling life, and how you can do the same.

PART ONE

INVEST IN YOURSELF

1

OWN YOUR SHIT

Living wild and free is fun at first. But It's not cute being broke, nor is it cute coming into work hungover and disheveled. It's not funny anymore when you can't hold down a job in your late twenties or early thirties. In fact, it's sad because it is totally preventable once you start taking responsibility for your own shit.

If you can't hold down a job for longer than a few months at a time, is it really always someone else's fault or does it reflect on your work ethic? If you're always in debt and can't seem to get out, is it the system or are you spending beyond your means? It's easy to blame others for our problems. It's much harder to look at your own faults and admit you're wrong.

Sure, you're not the stereotypical fuckup. But are you working at a job you hate in a career that's uninspiring? Do you complain about your job, boss or co-workers constantly? Do you feel helpless under your debt.

If so, it's time to stop bitching about it and do something to change it.

No one gives a shit about your problems -- except you. At some point, you have to reach a breaking point and want something more for yourself. Or you can accept leeching off of others and living paycheck to paycheck.

For me, change started happening during my mid-20s. At that age you start seeing people in your circle go in different directions: some focus on career or family, while others clutch desperately to the booze-filled glory days. You might get irritated by friends who no longer want to get drunk every weekend, or you might be admiring the people that are advancing in their careers and starting to purchase real estate, drive a decent car and go on real vacations.

This is also a time when people start losing touch, sometimes unintentionally, but sometimes deliberately. People will get tired of hearing your problems and the woe-is-me act. Friends don't want to be around negativity or hear your bitching anymore. After all, life is hard and everyone's got their shit.

Your mid-twenties are a major crossroads in life. It's a time when you have to decide what path you want to take: will you struggle through life going from self-inflicted crisis to crisis or will you take control?

I'm guessing you want the latter. Here's how to get it.

Get Honest With Yourself

The first step in taking control of your life is to do an honest evaluation of yourself. What are your strengths and weaknesses? What family patterns are you repeating? Where do you fall short?

It's not easy looking at your own faults, but it is necessary if you want to evolve and grow. Go for a walk, hit the gym or get outside and spend some time thinking about where you are and where you want to be. Then, grab a pen and paper and honestly answer the following questions:

- Am I using my time wisely?
- Am I taking anything or anyone for granted?
- Am I letting matters out of my hands stress me out?
- Am I always late?
- Do I have a hard time getting along with others?
- Am I putting enough effort into my relationships?

- Am I taking care of myself physically?
- Am I living true to myself?
- What am I doing about the things that matter most in my life?
- Have I done anything lately worth remembering?
- What do I need to change about myself?
- How do I want people to talk about me when I'm not in the room?
- Am I waking up ready to take on the day?

This is emotional heavy lifting, so you may want to give yourself a weekend to consider the questions, spacing them out and honestly answering a few at a time. Remember to be in depth and specific.

This exercise is important for everyone, and should be repeated regularly throughout your life. It allows you to look outside yourself and identify where you are struggling and where you are stuck in a rut. Once you can identify these points, you can begin to take steps to change your life.

Hear It How It Is

In order to really understand where you are, you need to look outside your own perspective and see how your actions affect others. That means it's time to find a friend, co-worker or family member that you know is honest to a fault. Buy them a drink or a meal, and ask them to be brutally honest. Use the questions above to steer your conversation, asking things like:

- Do you think I'm fulfilling my potential?
- What do you see as my biggest challenges?
- What words do my friends and loved ones use to describe me?

- What are my strengths?

An important note here: You are not allowed to get offended by any of the answers. If something hurts, it's probably what you need to hear. You need people in your life that can be honest with you, especially, if you're fucking up. You need someone to call you out on your bullshit every so often. And to get your shit together, you have to be secure enough to accept negative feedback and use it to get better.

Cultivating Conscientiousness

Once you've taken an honest inventory of where you are, it's time to make a plan for improvement. You want to live a successful life. Now, you have to decide how to get there.

Most people assume you have to be smart to be successful. However, intelligence is only a small part of what makes a person successful. Instead, personality has a huge impact on financial success. One personality trait is especially important: conscientiousness.

"Conscientious people tend to be super organized, responsible, and plan ahead. They work hard in the face of challenges and can control their impulses," Drake Baer writes for Business Insider.

Conscientiousness has been linked with higher salaries, better ability to hold a job and more job satisfaction, Baer writes. People who measure as highly conscientious have higher test scores, less disease and more success. That's what we all want, right?

Here are the traits that conscientious people have:

- Goal driven, and high achievers. Loves a challenge.
- Holds strong convictions. Certain.

- Hard-working and persevering.
- Neat, detailed and orderly. Often has a to-do list.
- Cautious and careful in all areas of their lives.
- Law-abiding and morally ethical. Does the "right thing."
- Highly satisfied with life.
- Reliable, responsible and honest.
- Able to manage conflict.
- Conservative; loves to follow the norm.

Now, you might be looking at this list thinking "That's not me." After all, young people aren't generally known for these qualities. The good news is that conscientiousness can be intentionally cultivated. Just like you have developed your business skills you can develop a personality that is primed for success.

Start taking these steps today:

- Keep tidy. Start in your work area or on your desk.
- Set a schedule. Use technology and apps to remind you of deadlines and tasks.
- Get mindful. Apps like Headspace and 10% Happier can help you cultivate conscientiousness in just a few minutes a day.

Although these are small steps, they'll make a huge difference as you start to get your shit together.

2

GET THE HELP YOU NEED TO HELP YOURSELF

After you've taken an honest look at where you are today, it's time to start planning for where you want to be. Although you're the one who needs to do the work, it's important to ask for help along the way. As difficult as it is to identify our own faults and self-harming patterns of behavior, it is just as hard to open up and ask others for help. However, getting help will have huge personal and professional benefits.

Part of your self reflection should be to identify whether or not you need help (spoiler alert: you do). The next step is to figure out what kind of help you need. Look at the journaling you did, and see what areas are problematic for you. *Are you partying too much? Getting bogged down by negative friends? Spending too much time dealing with demons in your own head?*

It's time to get that shit sorted, and reaching out for help is your first step.

Make Mental Health A Priority

We all know the benefits of going to the gym and taking care of ourselves physically. However, mental health is just as important -- maybe even more important -- for your success. According to the National Alliance on Mental Illness (NAMI), 1 in 5 American adults have a mental illness. Struggling with depression or other mental health conditions can cripple your productivity at work. In fact, mental illness causes $193.2 billion in lost earnings each year.

That's a pretty stunning number. Imagine how much more successful we could be as a society if people were proactive about managing their mental health, rather than letting mental illness derail their career trajectories.

No one wants to talk about mental illness, because it's so stigmatized. However, taking an honest look at your mental health is essential for success.

I know, because I have been there. I have struggled with anxiety and depression (along with some ADD) all throughout my adulthood. One day I found myself in the Emergency Room convinced I was dying. Really, I was having a panic attack, brought on by the depression and anxiety I had been trying to ignore.

In that moment my life changed, because I realized I needed professional help. Now, 15 years later, I don't recognize that person anymore because I've grown and evolved so much. I now use tools (including medication) to deal with stress and anxiety; I recognize triggers to my negative patterns; and I see mental health professionals regularly. That's not a weakness -- it's an investment in my health that makes me strong and more successful.

A mental health professional can help you recognize negative patterns of behavior and develop strategies to avoid them. They can make make you stronger and self aware as long as you are willing to put in the work. Mental health professionals have given me the tools to be better at relating to others, building the life I want for myself, and coping with the curve balls that life can throw my way -- in short, they've helped me get my shit together.

If you have health insurance, find out what's covered under your plan for mental health — counseling, medication, holistic therapy, rehab? How much will you have to pay out of pocket? Ask your primary care physician for referrals, get recommendations from friends, and research online to find mental health professionals who meet your needs and practice a type of therapy you're comfortable with.

Remember that there may be some trial and error in the process. You'll need several names, since some providers won't be taking new patients. You want to find a therapist who you connect with and can feel comfortable telling anything to without hesitation. Treat this process like an interview because your goal is to find someone that you can work with for the medium to long term. Don't be afraid to move on to someone else if you don't feel like you're clicking or it's not working for one reason or another. Therapy won't help unless you are completely honest and an active participant.

Take A Second Look At Substance Use

It can be nice to relax over a glass of wine or share a few beers with your buddies on the weekend. However, I've learned it's almost impossible to get your shit together if you're drinking too much. And the truth of the matter is many people are drinking (or smoking or using) too much: 9 percent of workers and 17 percent of unemployed people have a substance use disorder. As you work to get your shit together it's important to take an honest look at your substance use and how it is affecting your life.

When I was trying to ignore my anxiety and depression, I used alcohol to self medicate. Drinking started out as a fun social activity and another aspect of foodie culture for me to enjoy. But over time It shifted from a fun night out to using alcohol as an escape from life and the stress of being my dad's caretaker as he battled Alzheimer's for a decade.

I always knew I was drinking too much but I was still killing it at work, paying all the bills and doing my best as a husband and dad. Because of that, I felt that my drinking was manageable, but as the years passed I started gaining weight and having less energy. My overall health was declining.

Then, the Sunday after Thanksgiving in 2017, I started having severe abdominal pain that I thought was a digestive issue. The pain was debilitating and wasn't getting better. After a trip to my doctor's office and some blood work I got a call from my doctor. She said I needed to get to my nearest hospital because I was suffering from acute pancreatitis, an inflammation that kills as many as ten percent of people who have it and can increase risk of pancreatic cancer.

I sat in the hospital for four long days, missing work and my family -- the things I had convinced myself weren't affected by my alcohol use. I was on fluids and pain medications and unable to eat for three days. My doctor was brutally honest: she told me years of heavy drinking had triggered my hospital visit, and if I didn't stop, it was going to get worse.

My wife and I had learned that day that we were expecting our second child. I was determined never to be in this physical pain and leave my family hanging again, so I committed to stop drinking. I understood why this was important, but I didn't know how hard it was going to be to cut alcohol out of my life. I had to learn how to socialize without alcohol and how to use other, healthier tools to manage my stress.

Today I've been sober for over a year. Ditching alcohol has changed my life for the better: I weigh less, have more energy and am happier. I share this because it's important to realize that you don't have to be an alcoholic on the street for substance use to have negative effects on your life. Even if you're functioning well enough, like I was, it's likely that you could be achieving even more if you reduce your substance use.

Today, more and more people are realizing the benefits of sobriety. Groups like Sober(ish) and Hello Sunday Morning can help you reevaluate your substance use without committing to lifelong sobriety. There are even sober dance parties like Daybreaker that deliver the adrenaline rush of the club scene without the hangover. Why not try taking a break from alcohol and other substance, and see how that can change your life?

Form Your Team

Finding professional help and connecting with organizations like gyms or sobriety groups to support your growth are important. Next, it's time to take a look at who you're surrounding yourself with. The people around you will have a huge effect on your personal and professional life.

Mentors are invaluable to your professional growth. Having mentors early in my career directly impacted my current success. I was lucky to get mentored by some of the best in my field and apply their lessons to my life everyday.

Mentors share their experiences in order to teach you lessons beyond the concrete skills that you learn in school or work training. Practical experience teaches you "soft" skills that are essential to succeed -- things like communications, relationship building and personality traits that will help you in your field. These include professionalism, interpersonal skills, and leadership and management skills. Today, when many young people spend more time on technology and less time building face-to-face relationships, a good mentor who can help you develop these soft skills is more important than ever.

So how and where should you find mentors? Find mentors through the people you are working with and interacting with already. Realistically, you need a relationship with someone in order for them to want to spend time mentoring you.

I was lucky that I was an assistant for three top-performing sales professionals, who were generous in passing on their knowledge and will to show me how to do things the right way. Mentorship should happen organically in your career.

Sheryl Sandberg writes in her book *Lean In*, "If someone has to ask the question, the answer is probably no. When someone finds the right mentor, it is obvious. The question becomes a statement. Chasing or forcing that connection rarely works."

It's also key to remember that mentorship is a give and take relationship between mentor and mentee. Successful people get inundated with requests of all kinds all day long. They will want to know how you operate and what motivates you, in order to determine whether or not you're worth their time investment.

In order to get on the radar of strangers you admire, support and help their work. Engage with them on social media. Refer people to them, share their posts and further their conversation. Give, give and give. That way, people will want to return the favor. Remember, it's a two way street and this is a great way to get noticed.

Ask yourself if you're a good mentee candidate. Would you want to mentor yourself if the roles were flipped? Are you open minded, willing to take direction, respectful, and able to take responsibility?

Here are a few ways to present yourself as a good project for a mentor:

- Demonstrate your value by actively building your career. Get noticed by being great at what you do or show great promise if you're not there yet.
- Ask for more responsibility in areas that you feel you can contribute. Offer to train the new hire or summarize the meeting you were part of. Add value.
- Volunteer to represent your team on inter-departmental initiatives or industry groups. Support and help others succeed.

Outside work, surround yourself with people who are going to support you. Think back to your reflection and consider your relationships:

- Are the people you spend time with positive? Happy? Do they have their shit together?
- Do they make you feel like you have what it takes to reach your goals?
- Do they support your goals?
- Are they ambitious and passionate about life?
- Do you feel happy and energized after you spent time with them?

If you're not answering "yes" for your existing friends it's time to foster new, more positive relationships. It can be difficult to distance yourself from people you've known your whole life, start by doing it in small steps. People grow apart in life for a reason. At the same time, intentionally seek out social opportunities at groups like bowling leagues, fantasy sports leagues, trivia nights, book clubs, young professionals clubs, etc.

Nobody gets anywhere in life by themselves. Every billionaire, CEO or champion has had mentors, friends, family who support them along the way. It takes a village. Who are you bringing into yours?

3

SELF CARE

"When the well's dry, we know the worth of water."
- Benjamin Franklin

How many of us run ourselves ragged on a regular basis? My days usually go something like this: Wake up early, get the kids ready, get them to school, inhale a protein bar and coffee on the way into work, work 8 hours (or more if there's a deadline coming up), pick the kids up from school and activities, make and eat dinner, get the kids to bed, maybe do a little a little laundry. Then, collapse into bed, usually later than I should.

It's *exhausting*.

Most of us have a lot going on: we grind at work and show up for our loved ones. While saying yes to everything and everyone can seem important, eventually our tanks go empty and stress takes its toll. That's when you come down with a flu, migraine, ulcer, or another stress-related ailment, and then you're no good to anybody. The effects of stress are well documented and include everything from catching more colds (since stress lowers your immune system), developing heart disease, or battling insomnia or depression.

If you're trying to get your shit together, you need to put yourself first. It's said that you can't pour from an empty cup. In order to be able to give to others -- personally or professionally -- you have to have something left for yourself.

In recent years "self-care" has become a buzzword, but it

doesn't have to be complicated to make a big difference in your life. I strive to make sure my self care is spread over three areas: physical, mental and mindfulness. These areas are all equally important to success, and you'll be running like a well oiled machine if you have them working in harmony.

Mental Health Matters

We already talked about the importance of reaching out for help from mental health professionals when you need it. However, maintaining good mental health goes well beyond that.

This past year has been full of major, stressful life events for me. I was hospitalized with pancreatitis and got sober. My father died, my second son was born, and my brother was diagnosed with cancer. With my on-and-off struggle with depression and anxiety I knew that I was in danger of falling into a very dark place.

Because of that, I doubled down on caring for my mental health. There have been low points and long stretches of emotional pain, but it's also been a year of deep reflection and processing. My saving grace has been all of the work I've done, and continue to, on my mental and emotional health. This means not just keeping up with counseling and medications, but also focusing on the non-drug related "prescriptions," every mental health professional recommends: exercise, nutrition, and good quality sleep. This is part of a holistic approach for wellbeing and living an active positive life.

I can't even imagine what mental space I would be in if I hadn't learned tools from a mental health professional in my early twenties. Getting professional help saved my life, and prioritizing mental health has led me to a more well adjusted life and stable career.

Focus On Physical Fitness

If you're in your 20's, you might be lucky enough to still experience a breakneck metabolism that keeps you thin. But that doesn't mean that you should skip the gym. Exercise has a shitload of benefits besides looking great in your suit. It can add to your physique, help you lose weight, and improve your sex life; but most importantly it can give you a sense of wellbeing.

Today, adults spend too much time sitting, don't eat healthy enough, and are increasingly isolated from others. I do love a good Netflix binge, but humans are not supposed to be sedentary. The 'fight or flight' instinct we have needs a physical outlet to release that energy; if we don't have that, it manifests into anxiety and depression.

Exercising three times a week can reduce your risk for depression and also increase your brain plasticity and health, meaning you'll be extra sharp in your next meeting. Plus, team sports can be a great networking opportunity.

Carve out time in your daily routine for movement. You don't have to be lifting huge weights or running a new personal record time. Just going for a walk (especially outside), playing a pickup game of basketball or swimming laps can have great benefits for your overall health, which will help you perform at a higher level in all areas of your life. And remember -- if you pick an activity you love (for me that was basketball), you'll be more likely to stick to your exercise routine.

Exercise also helps you sleep better, and sleep is critical for success. Get a good mattress, cut the screen time and work toward getting 8 hours of uninterrupted sleep.

Get Mindful

Like self-care, mindfulness has become a buzzword. Despite how often it is mentioned, many people don't really understand what mindfulness is. According to the Mayo Clinic, "Mindfulness is the act of being intensely aware of what you're sensing and feeling at every moment – without interpretation or judgment."

Mindfulness is the ability to be fully aware of the present without being overwhelmed or reactive. It can be done during meditation, exercise or yoga. Science proves that mindfulness has huge benefits, including reducing stress, improving memory, and stabilizing emotions.

Mindfulness is challenging for me. My brain goes a mile a minute grappling with thoughts spurred by my anxiety, ADD and depression. It's important for me to be able to slow my brain down in order to think clearly. Practicing mindfulness has help me with with problem solving, creative thinking and strategy -- all of which make me a more successful businessman.

Today there are tons of apps to help you increase your mindfulness. One of my favorite is Headspace, which offers guided meditations for just ten minutes a day. Give their free trial a go and see if it makes a difference for you.

Take Some Time Off

When we want to achieve more we're told to *lean in*, *just do it*, or keep grinding. We live in a corporate culture where taking extended vacation has a negative connotation. The awful truth is that we all judge our co-workers, colleagues, employers, when they take time off frequently or take more than one week off at a time. We all think, "Must be nice..."

The truth is, it's more than nice -- it can also be a sound business decision. People who take time to relax and recharge are more productive, research shows. Their quality of work and output is higher than the people who work long hours and don't take vacation. In fact, research suggests that that if Americans took more vacation our economy would benefit.

These ideas are slowly catching on in the American workplace. Companies ranging from Dropbox to StitchFix are experimenting with offering their employees unlimited vacation days. In Europe, countries like The Netherlands are experimenting with four-day work week. Data suggests that employees can get as much accomplished in four days as they currently do in five, and people often feel more relaxed and fulfilled when they work fewer hours.

Of course, how time off is handled will depend on the company you work for. It's hard to take time off if your superiors will frown on it. However, remember that taking time away from the office is often good for you personally and professionally. At the very least, be sure to use the vacation time that you're entitled to.

While vacations are great, they're also rare. That's why it's important to embrace mini breaks. Begin working these moments of peace and relaxation into your schedule throughout the week and you'll be surprised to see how much more relaxed and energized you feel. This week try to incorporate a one of these mini break activities into each day:

- Go for a walk
- Meditate
- Go out for lunch
- Read a book
- Take a 15 minute break to jam out to your favorite tunes
- Go to the gym

In order for you to achieve financial and professional success you need a strong foundation, self-understanding and health. Self-care helps you cultivate these things. The better we care for ourselves, the more we can accomplish, so make it a priority to sit down and plan time for self care throughout the week. You'll be surprised how much this help you get your shit together.

4

PLANNING FOR THE FUTURE

What are you working toward? Sure, you want to get your shit together. But in order to actually do that you need to define what you want to accomplish. Without your destination defined, it's impossible to know what road you should be traveling. That's where planning for the future comes in.

Before you get started setting goals willy nilly, you need to ask yourself some deep and important questions: *What is important to you? Is it money? Prestige? What are your core values? What drives you? Are you satisfied with a roof over your head, food and a little bit of fun money? Do you just need a paycheck from work, or do you want a job that gives you emotional and intellectual fulfillment as well?*

More importantly, what do you want to accomplish with this life? After all, you only get one chance.

Set Goals

Once you know what you want to accomplish in life, you can start working toward that by setting goals. The more manageable and specific a goal is the more likely you are to accomplish it. "Be happy," is an admirable goal, but it doesn't give much definition for what that looks like.

When I am setting goals for myself I like to divide them into personal and professional goals. Then, I consider what I want to accomplish in the short, medium and long term. Your short term goals should lead you to your medium term goals and eventually to your long term goals. Once you've structured your goals this way, you've defined your destination and the stops you need to make along the way -- in short, you have a road map to success. Now all you have to do is get moving.

Here are tips for setting and accomplishing goals:

- **Take it one step at a time.** Focus on one goal and finish that before moving onto the next. It's better to start slowly than to have unfinished tasks bogging you down.
- **Write down your goal and action plan.** An action plan of clearly defined, small steps will keep you moving towards your goals. Write your action plan down and keep it nearby. In order to really understand what you'll have to do, ask mentors, do research and talk to colleagues. We have the tools to connect with one another -- use them!
- **Give yourself a deadline.** Once you've made an action plan, set due dates for each step of the plan. You can adjust these along the way, but having a deadline will give you motivation to put in the necessary work.

These three steps make even the most lofty goals look manageable. For example, your long-term goal might be to be a millionaire. Focusing on that as a broke 20-something can be disheartening. However, putting together a budget and breaking down how much money you can save and invest on a month to month basis is tangible and manageable progress toward that goal. With those baby steps you won't get paralyzed into inaction when something seems too big.

The key to successful goal setting is focusing on the details.

Compounding doesn't only apply to money: tiny daily actions compound to massive results. Success doesn't come from one big move, it is a result of small consistent actions over time. Despite what pop culture says, nobody becomes an overnight success.

Instead of dreaming of your big break, be consistent and relentless in your pursuit of excellence. Mindfulness practice comes in handy here because it's important to stay in the moment. Focus on the now, because that is the only time you can affect. Then, watch yourself check off your goals and work toward those big-picture accomplishments.

Educate Yourself

In school I was average. Yet, today I earn more money than most of the kids in my class. Being a straight A student doesn't guarantee financial success. Yes, it certainly takes a level of discipline and effort to consistently get good grades, but your GPA does not measure the emotional intelligence or creative problem solving skills that you need to succeed in the real world.

Ultimately, you need to be able to translate those skills and work ethic into money. How do you do that? Do something that people are willing to pay for. The real key is to get people to pay over and over again. That means whatever you do or sell needs to make whoever's buying consistently happy.

If you have big plans to get your shit together and become financially independent, you need to be better than the competition. You must fill a need that's not being met in your marketplace or provide something that improves a customer's life. To do this you need to educate yourself, not necessarily by attending school, but by constantly seeking opportunities to learn.

For me, school provided a baseline of knowledge and curiosity, but my most important education came after I graduated and was tossed into the "real" world. I learned important life skills like understanding my brain, processing emotions and using positive outlets. I realized that while subjects like history and math might be useful, learning how to present yourself properly is a key to success.

To be successful, you must learn to:

- Show up on time.
- Work hard.
- Communicate effectively in all forms.
- Master time management.
- Foster interpersonal relationships .
- Know how to influence and motivate someone to make a purchase decision.
- Understand how to manage money and make it work for you.
- Plan strategically for your future.
- Utilize networking opportunities.
- Be likable.
- Negotiate effectively.
- Market yourself effectively.

Some of these skills are universally accepted as important. I was motivated to pursue them because I understood that they would help me make money and get closer to achieving financial freedom.

However, some of these skills you might think you don't need. If you're not in sales, for example, do you really need to know how to influence a purchase decision? Yes, you do. All business interactions require these skills and having them will help you outperform the competition.

For example, consider two freelance web developers with equal skill and knowledge of the marketplace. Yet, one markets herself better. She is more likeable and professional. She meets deadlines and does more than is asked. She responds in a timely fashion and is an effective communicator. That individual will earn more than her competition. It's not good enough to be a skilled web developer in this scenario -- it's the other stuff that gets you hired and paid.

Intentionally Fostering New Skills

To reach your potential and achieve your goals you need to educate yourself. And just like school required effort (whether you were getting straight A's or not), continuing your education requires work. However, unlike your school days, learning opportunities won't fall into your lap in the real world. Instead, you need to constantly seek them out. Here's how:

Read

Remember your teacher in elementary school telling you reading is the key to success? Turns out, she was right. Many ultra-successful individuals are voracious readers. Warren Buffett once said, "Read 500 pages like this every day. That's how knowledge works. It builds up, like compound interest. All of you can do it, but I guarantee not many of you will do it." He famously devotes most of his day to reading.

He isn't the only one. Bill Gates reads a book a week. Elon Musk is an avid reader. When asked how he learned to build rockets, he said, "I read books."

But there are no light reads or trashy novels here. The ultra-wealthy read specifically to educate themselves.

Reading is such a powerful form of education because it's free and easy to do. Join the local library and you have instant access to a wealth of information. Then, you can just start working slowly through it: If you read 10 pages a day over the

365 days in a year, you'll have read 3,650 pages. That's a lot of information.

Some of you may be thinking, "Who has the time?" I get it. I have kids and have a demanding job, and most days the only thing I want to do at night is veg out to Netflix. But if we're being honest there's no reason not to dedicate ten minutes a day to reading. It's a small effort, but can have huge reward. Remember what Buffett said: All of your reading compounds over time like interest. Your brain connects all of this knowledge to form new solutions and creativity, all of which help you succeed. Plus, new research shows that reading can reduce stress, depression, and dementia, and increase happiness and fulfillment.

Listen

Listening is never a bad idea. And today, we have more opportunities than ever to learn by listening thanks to audiobooks and podcasts. These audio options deliver the same information as books, with the benefit of being easily accessible. Long ride to work? Why not listen to that new podcast? Hitting the gym? Perfect time to engage with a new TED Talk. Just like reading, these audio options expose you to new information and ideas that are critical for growing and educating.

Look

There's a lot of junk online, but there's also heaps of information. E-learning courses, Youtube tutorials, and blogs offer free, accessible education that you can go through at your own pace. The digital revolution has given billions of people access to learning anything they want.

Digital learning opportunities, both formal and informal, have major advantages, including:

- Flexibility. E-learning can be done at a time that works best for the student. I try to do it after the kids go to bed and I have a little mental capacity left.
- Access: You can re-watch lessons and lectures as many times as you want.
- Up to date information: Online resources are often updated in real time.
- Efficient: Today you don't have to drive to class or sit through lectures on topics you're not interested in. Instead, you can hone in on the skills that are most important to you.
- Low Cost. With public college costing more than $25,000 and private schools charging double that, free education online is more appealing than ever. You can learn, without acquiring student debt.

Talk

Today there's a temptation to do everything ourselves. After all, you can access a world of education without even leaving your bed. However, it's important not to forget how personal relationships are critical for your education.

Having respected peers and mentors to talk to is critical. With these people you can bounce ideas off, vent, and get guidance. They're not your boss, so they can give you an unbiased opinion. They can see areas you need to work on and give you an outside perspective. They can nudge you in the right direction when you need it and get you out of your negative thoughts. Oftentimes, you may not realize the importance of these relationships until years later.

5

CONNECT WITH LIKE-MINDED PEOPLE

One of the most important steps to turning your life around is surrounding yourself with like minded people. We've touched on this in previous chapters, but it's worth reiterating because it's just so important. If you want to really get your shit together, surround yourself with people who are further ahead in their careers and financial journeys than you are.

You've probably seen the quote, "When a flower doesn't bloom you fix the environment in which it grows, not the flower." If you want to grow, you need to cut everything and everyone out of your life that will deter you from achieving your goals, and spend time with people who support your goals.

Research suggests that powerful emotions like happiness and anger are contagious -- so much so that researchers can track their progress through a town. Because of this, it's important you think about not just the people who are in your life the most, but also the people who are on the fringes. After all, those negative coworkers could be having a real toll on your growth.

Changing Your Environment

The first thing you should do is to take an honest look at your life and who you spend it with. In order to make big changes, you need to analyze your habits and social circles carefully and make decisions based on your conclusions.

Try this experiment: carry a journal with you everywhere you go. Write down how you feel after interactions with people in your life, how you feel after you eat a shitty meal, how you feel after a long night out at the bar. Do this for a month to get a decent sample size.

When that's over, re-read your notes. Identify who and what made you feel lousy and do the same for what makes you feel good. You'll likely come to the realization that some of your friends, family and coworkers are negative people that drain your body and mind of energy.

So what do we do with this information?

Start to distance yourself from toxic people in your life. Don't engage with people who try to control you, pay no attention to your boundaries or make excuses for their actions. Stay away from habitual liars and "victims." These people are not the soil you want to grow in.

This step is difficult but necessary. It will take time and might get ugly. You could find yourself 'breaking up' with friends you've known for years. Unless they're also ready to get their shit together, they probably won't understand why you're not mixing it up at the bar regularly anymore or listening to another story about how the world is conspiring against them.

Next, take the same inventory of your your lifestyle and habits. Figure out how many hours of sleep you need to be productive. How are you eating habits? Are you working out enough to get your feel good chemicals generating in your brain? How much tv are you watching? How much time do you waste scrolling through social media? Look back on your journal and do more of the things that fill you up, and less of the activities that drain you. Normalize success by being around it all the time.

Building The Right Environment

Once you've taken an honest look at your friends, acquaintances and habits, and distanced yourself from the people and things that are bringing you down, it's time to build your new, more positive environment.

One of the hardest parts is connecting with like-minded people. Once you're out of school you have to make an effort to meet new people. Start with local groups. Anything from professional networking events to 12-step meetings or sports clubs can do the trick. Just focus on surrounding yourself with people who have similar goals as you.

Once you're comfortable in a group, find a mentor who is further along in their journey than you to provide you with guidance.

The first step toward finding a mentor is working hard and developing a reputation for being successful. Promising young talent is hard to find and powerful people are constantly on the lookout for it. Build a personal reputation of being motivated, teachable, curious, talented and reliable.

If you build it, they will come.

The best place to start looking for a mentor is in your professional circle. Consider old bosses, former teachers, coworkers in other departments and family or friends. Prioritize people who can help you with your long-term goals. Remember that a mentor relationship should be grown organically, and you need to give before asking for anything. Make yourself worth someone's time.

Nobody is truly 'self-made.' There were teachers, advisors, friends, mentors, family, who helped them along the way. Whether it was a gentle nudge from a teacher to pursue an interest or a friend who tells you when you're fucking up, getting help along the way is essential to success.

It's important to make yourself an appealing mentee.

Remember that your mentor is giving freely of his or her time, effort and knowledge. Respect that, bring something to the table where you can, and honor your commitments. No one wants to spend their time trying to help a flake.

Just as importantly, know your goals and share them with your mentor. If you can present a clearly defined vision of what your goals are people are more willing to help you achieve them, because they can see you've taken initiative to start the process.

Give Back To Others

Once you've surrounded yourself with positive people and a great mentor, it's time to give back. You don't need to wait till you've "made it" to make a difference for others. Celebrate the success of others, welcome newcomers to your club and share knowledge when you can.

Being of service to others is good for you, too. It will also force you to reflect and re-evaluate your priorities in life. Mentoring is therapeutic and a fulfilling distraction from your own life. It will recalibrate your mindset and help you see things differently. You might even find new energy being around someone new to the game.

PART TWO

MAKE MONEY

6

HOW TO MAXIMIZE YOUR EARNED INCOME

Most of us go to work each and every day, and collect a paycheck every week or two. It's the daily grind, and it's how most of us spend our careers: earning income. Earned income is money that you make when you're actively working for wages, commission or tips. Whether you're self employed or have an employer, earned income is the main source of money for most people.

Most of us want to earn more money. If you're self-employed you have the option to work more hours or raise your rates. However, if you work for someone else, things are less in your control: your employer puts a price on your time based on how much revenue you generate, and that's the price they pay you.

There are two obvious ways to maximize your income. You can ask for a raise (just make sure you can explain why you've earned it). Or, you can work more (more hours, more projects or more deals closed, depending on your pay structure).

These are fairly obvious, but there are other ways to maximize your earned income throughout your career. Here are a few things to consider early on in your career:

Choose The Right Career

How often have you been told to pursue your passion? I'm here to tell you that if you want to get your shit together (and keep it that way) you need to ignore that advice.

That's right: ignore it. Toss out every guru and Google search that said following your passion will make you millions. There are many athletes and artists who will tell you that isn't the case. And now, science is starting to back them up.

Last year, researchers at Stanford decided to look at this well-intentioned career advice, and determine -- to be frank -- it sucks.

The study found that rather than pursuing your passion, you need to develop it. I didn't get into sales because I was passionate about it, but over time I developed a passion for it.

So, what's so bad about following your passion? The researchers found that people who were told to follow their passions were more apt to quit when the going got tough. After all, following your passion is supposed to be easy, right?

"Mantras like 'find your passion' carry hidden implications," the researchers wrote. "They imply that once an interest resonates, pursuing it will be easy."

Researchers found that people who believe that that passion can be cultivated over time were more open minded, something that is critical in today's job market. After all, progress happens when diverse ideas intersect and people are able to use different perspectives to find solutions.

The authors of the article recommend that you develop a passion instead of chasing the most obvious choice. Billionaire Mark Cuban agrees. He once said, "One of the great lies of life is 'Follow your passions.' I used to be passionate to be a baseball player. Then I realized I had a 70-mile-per-hour fastball."

When Cuban realized his big league dreams were dead, he was able to foster business skills, and with time business became his passion. As he became better at it, he was even more interested.

"When you look at where you put in your time, where you put in your effort, that tends to be the things that you are good at. And if you put in enough time, you tend to get really good at it," Cuban said. "If you put in enough time, and you get really good, I will give you a little secret: Nobody quits anything they are good at, because it is fun to be good. It is fun to be one of the best."

This has been true for me. I became passionate about sales because I was able to develop the skill at work over time. When I finished college I had no idea what I wanted to do. By chance, I started as a sales assistant at a growing international company. My job was to support three sales reps by doing their administrative work so they could focus more time to sales and face time with customers. This was my main source of income so I took it seriously, especially since I had the added motivation of wanting to move out of my dad's house.

I started earning $50,000 per year, which was pretty good in 2005 for a new grad with little experience. As happy as I was with my paycheck and newfound independence, I was really intrigued when I realized how much money our sales reps made off commission. With their commission checks they made even more than their managers. I worked hard and showed initiative, hoping to get an opportunity in sales. Once I got a shot, I never looked back. Fourteen years later, I'm the top sales rep at the company and have been for the last four out of five years.

So my advice is this: don't fret about finding what your passion is in order to determine your career path. Instead, immerse yourself into a skill that matches your strengths.

Take a career survey and personality test like the Myers-Briggs Type Indicator. This screening helps identify if you are extroverted or introverted, how you take in information, how you make decisions (logically or emotionally) and whether you like to reach decisions quickly or are more likely to stay open to new ideas. There is also the Career Personality Profiler, a scientifically-proven career test that measures your personality traits and interests in order to find the right career.

Be open minded and continually develop your skills. Remember: it's fun being good at something. It's even more fun to be the best.

And remember -- maximizing your earned income can help you spend more time on the things you really are passionate about. My dad started his career at 13 in a shoe factory because he lived in post-WWII Germany, and my grandmother knew someone there who could get him a job. It became a passion of his because it helped support his family and felt good to be great at something. He became a lifelong shoe maker, which, afforded him a very comfortable life. In turn, he could pursue his other passions -- including traveling, tracking down his family history, and spending time with his family.

All because of shoes, which he had no idea would become his passion until he actually started doing it.

The point is, none of us really know what we'll end up doing in life. The important thing is to be open and get experience trying different things. Who knows, you might surprise yourself.

Market Yourself

Whether you're self-employed or salaried, how you market yourself is critical. Here, again, it's important to identify the skills you have. Remember, they don't have to be perfect -- you can develop these skills over time.

Ask yourself what comes easily to you that others struggle with? For example, can you make conversation with anyone? Do you always have a creative solution? Are you a whiz at organizing?

Decide what your skills are, and who you are marketing yourself to. This might be your boss or freelance clients, for example. Then, present yourself to those people as a solution to a problem they have. Remember, when you're marketing yourself you want to convince people that you can make their lives easier or more efficient -- and that you're worth the money they'll pay.

Know What You're Good At

Following your passion may not be great advice. However, making money by doing things that come easy to you is great advice. Today it's easy to make money at something you're good at and enjoy. For example, if you enjoy being around dogs, look into working at a doggie day care or use services like Rover to get paid walking dogs. If you're an artist, look into teaching art classes at a local studio.

We live in a world with more opportunity than ever to maximize income because the barriers of entry have been greatly reduced. The internet has allowed musicians to gain direct access to the marketplace and not rely on record labels anymore; TV executives now look for talent on Youtube; writers can land book deals through a viral post. If you have access to the internet through a smartphone, you really have no excuse.

Of course, when it comes to maximizing earned income, the skills we talked about in part one are essential. You need to set clear goals. Decide what career path you want to take (corporate, entrepreneur, gig economy). Then, put a plan together and take actionable steps. Remember, consistent action leads to consistent results. Consistency is about taking small steps daily that help move you toward your highest priorities and goals.

Maximize Your Income

While the big-picture steps above are important, there are also concrete steps you can take to increase your earnings over your lifetime. These include:

Negotiate your salary

Negotiating your salary can make the biggest difference in your lifetime earning potential. According to a Career Builder survey, approximately half of workers don't negotiate their salaries because they feel uncomfortable asking for more money. Sound familiar?

On the flip side, half of the employers who participated in the survey report that their first offer is a lowball offer. A quarter of those lowball offers are reportedly $5,000 less than what employers expect to ultimately pay. A $5,000 dollar difference makes a huge impact on your lifetime earnings, especially since all of your raises and job offers will be based off your previous income level. If you leave this $5,000 on the table, so to speak, you will be losing hundreds of thousands of dollars over the course of your career. Negotiating your salary and raises throughout your career might be your biggest opportunity to maximize your lifetime earnings.

Before getting to the negotiating table, do your homework and know what other employers are paying for your position on sites like Glassdoor. Know what you're worth and don't settle for anything less.

Be Indispensable

One of the main reasons people are uncomfortable asking for more money is a lack of confidence. So how can you build your confidence?

Get better at what you do and become a "go-to" person at work. The better you get and the more your employer, team and clients rely on you, the more indispensable you become. When you're indispensable, your value to the company increases.

Additionally, word gets out when you become a star and you will start to get offered higher salaries as people try to recruit you. You may even get a signing bonus. Knowing that you're wanted by other companies gives you the confidence to ask for things, because you know you could get them somewhere else.

Getting better at your job means diving into it fully, soaking up as much knowledge as you can from managers, trainers and mentors, and studying, taking classes or reading books that can help you get better. It's not rocket science, but it does take planning, effort and initiative. However, it will pay off in the long term.

Get a Side-Hustle

You've negotiated your salary and are getting better at your job. You might be maxing out your income with your employer but you want to make more. A side hustle is a great way to supplement your income, and there are more ways than ever to earn extra cash in our gig economy.

A 2017 Bankrate survey found more than 44 million Americans have a side hustle and almost 40 percent of people with a side-gig earn $500 or more per month. That money can be used to pay down student loan debt, make extra payments to pay down your mortgage or save up enough to invest in passive income streams. When you account for the decreased interest and return on investment, your side hustle can pay big.

Consider this: Investing $6,000 a year (maximum contribution allowed in 2019) in an IRA retirement account over 30 years and earning an average 7 percent return would leave you with a nest egg of $652,111.78. That's amazing money for a side-hustle!

It's up to you to decide what you're willing and able to do to maximize your earnings. Some of you may decide to drive for Uber or Lyft or some of you may feel more comfortable walking dogs through Rover. Whatever you choose, make sure it's something you're willing to commit to because life is too short to spend all your time hating whatever it is you're doing.

Invest in Your Education

Investing in your education can be expensive if you take out loans for degrees that don't traditionally pay out in the "real world." However, investing in your education wisely can increase your lifetime earnings substantially. Consider these statistics from the US Bureau of Labor Statistics:

- **Average Salary With A High School Diploma**
    - Median annual earnings for workers with a high school are $35,256 per year. The current unemployment rate for those with a high school diploma is 5.4%.
- **Average Salary with an Associate Degree**
    - Median annual earnings for someone with an associate degree are $41,496 per year. The unemployment rate for those with an associate degree is 3.8%.
- **Average Salary with a Bachelor's Degree**
    - The average annual earnings for people with bachelor's degrees are $59,124 per year. The unemployment rate for those with bachelor's degrees is 2.8%.

- **Average Salary with a Master's Degree**
    - Median annual earnings for a master's degree is $69,732 per year. The unemployment rate for these workers averages 2.4%.
- **Average Salary with a Professional Degree**
    - Workers with a professional degree have the highest annual income, averaging $89,960 per year, with the lowest unemployment rate of 1.5%.

The bottom line is that your educational level will have an impact on your lifetime earnings. However, traditional education isn't for everyone so there is no need to panic. Earning more from your job doesn't necessarily translate to more retirement income. Earn the most you can but be smart with your budgeting and invest wisely.

Also, if you have to take out expensive student loans, it'll take you much longer to build your wealth. Look into community colleges and state schools for a more cost effective way to achieve your financial goals.

Apply for that New Job

In corporate America it's common to get "stuck" on the corporate ladder. You are great at your job and have communicated your career ambitions to management. And yet, nothing has happened and you don't see upward opportunities anytime soon.

If this is you, it may be time to start looking for a change in employment. The average raise when starting a new job is 10-20%.

Before you start searching for new opportunities, optimize your LinkedIn profile and update your resume. Don't be afraid to apply for jobs that you don't think you're totally qualified for. Be confident with what you can bring to the table.

Remember, the money you earn today can be put to work to build passive income streams (more on that in a later chapter). Because of that, it's a great idea to work hard to optimize your earned income.

7

CREATE A BUDGET FOR YOUR LIFE

It's great to maximize your income. But there is a cap on earned income: no matter how much you earn, there are only so many hours in a day that you can dedicate to work. Because there's a limit on the amount of money you're able to earn, it's very important to understand where your money is going. That's where budgeting comes in.

Now, people get uptight when we talk about budgeting. It can feel restrictive. However, you would never run a successful company without a budget, and you shouldn't run a successful life without one either. Consider what these high-wealth individuals say about budgeting:

"It's not how much money you make, but how much money you keep, how hard it works for you, and how many generations you keep it for."
— Robert Kiyosaki, author of "Rich Dad, Poor Dad."

"Financial peace isn't the acquisition of stuff. It's learning to live on less than you make, so you can give money back and have money to invest. You can't win until you do this."
— Dave Ramsey, financial educator.

"Money is a terrible master but an excellent servant."
— P.T. Barnum, showman and politician

You Don't Know What You Don't Know

Our educational system fails us in teaching about financial planning. As a result, many people leave school with no idea about the basics of finances. They fall into traps like high interest credit card debt, variable rate mortgages and payday loans. Or, they just spend money without thinking about what they're spending on and how they could establish healthier habits.

Some people blow off financial literacy because they don't understand it. But luckily, you don't have to be a math whiz to manage your money. Once you know the basics it's easy to keep your ducks in a line. The first and most important step is to remove shame around finances and be willing to learn.

At its core, budgeting is pretty simple — addition and subtraction. Keep more money than you spend. If your expenses are fixed and you want more money, you need to find a way to earn more. If you can cut some non-essential expenses and your income is fixed, you take home more money.

Some people become paralyzed when they try to learn about finances because there are many experts, each of whom espouses slightly different methods and details when it comes to budgeting. Just remember, no matter whose philosophy you follow, in the end, the goal is the same: Save and Invest more Money than you Spend.

A Budget That Works For You

Think of a budget like a roadmap to your financial destination. You have financial goals, and your budget is a step that will help you achieve them. Here, it's important to work with your significant other to make sure the whole family is on the same page.

Before you can start working toward your goals, you have

to define them. What are you saving and investing for? That's why the first question you should ask before you set a budget is:

- **What are my priorities in life?**

  List your priorities and goals in life. Once you run your numbers, you'll be able to see where you have room in your budget and create a definitive strategy to reach your goals.

  My priorities are: provide a safe stable home for my family; have financial flexibility in five years to make any career move I want; have enough money to spend on travel and experiences; retire when my youngest son turns 18. *What do your priorities look like?*

Next, it's time to talk about your numbers. Ask yourself:

- **What is my/our income?**

  This one is simple for most households that collect a regular paycheck. For others, including entrepreneurs, business-owners, freelancers or tip-based workers, it can be harder to predict. In these cases, take a conservative approach and average out your income for the last 12 months, or take the lowest income you've earned in a month. Don't include bonuses because they aren't guaranteed.

- **What do I owe?**

  What are your monthly debt payments? List your debts, including mortgage, car payments, student loans, credit cards, and anything else that you pay regularly. Write down the totals you owe on each debt, the interest rates, and the minimum monthly payment due.

- **What are my monthly expenses?**

  These are your monthly expenses that aren't debts. They include rent, subscriptions, insurance and utility bills. First, list recurring payments like gym memberships and phone bills. Then, list variable and discretionary spending like groceries, entertainment, dining out, shopping and vacation.

- **What needs to change?**

  This question is the moment of reckoning. Ideally, your incomings should exceed your outgoings. If not, you're taking on debt every month. However, what you really want is for your income to exceed your expenses, preferably by a lot. If it doesn't, think about what you need to change.

  The benefit of writing everything out is that you can visualize everything. What debts should you pay down faster? What expenses can I cut or reduce? Do you need to earn more income?

- **How can I keep this sustainable?**

  Here, think about the first question -- your priorities. Consider how your current budget aligns with those, and make adjustments to get them into better alignment. For example, since I want to retire in 18 years, I plan on paying down most of the principal on my mortgage because this is our largest monthly expense. I also plan on having enough passive income to cover basic expenses, and enough saved and invested to last my wife and I until we are 90.

All this being said, setting budgets take personal sacrifice. Remember, cutting back can help you get your shit together.

You might have to give up your daily Starbucks run or going out with your friends on weekends. Are you ready for it?

Although finances weren't my main motivation for quitting drinking, not going out has left me with more money each month. I found free, healthier alternatives, like starting my Layupforlife blog, making working out a priority again and reading more. Sticking to a budget can be a daunting task, but will be well worth the effort in the long term.

8

PUT YOUR MONEY TO WORK

"Many folks think they aren't good at earning money, when what they don't know is how to use it."
— Frank A. Clark, politician

"I personally feel that the #1 benefit of having my expenses covered by passive income is that I get to keep doing a lot more of the kind of work I enjoy. I also get to work the way I want to work — where I want, when I want, how I want, and with whom I want."
— Steve Pavlina, personal development expert.

Earned income (also known as active income) is when you work and are paid for that work. If you have a job, you get paid based on the work that you do. If you leave that job, you stop getting paid -- and since we only have a finite number of hours in the day, there's a limit to how much active income you can generate.

Get your shit together and you can set up another source of money: passive income. Passive income is when you get paid whether you are actively working or not. Sounds pretty appealing, right?

Most of us have some sort of passive income, like the interest in our savings account. However, there are other, larger sources of passive income that can really change your life, like dividend and interest payments, rent collected from properties you own, and royalties from your creative works.

There's this idea that passive income is free money, but that's not quite true. Passive income is a result of a lot of front-loaded work on investments, which will pay you back later. Don't make the mistake of thinking that establishing passive income does not involve work. It takes upfront effort, time and strategy to create a reliable passive income stream.

Focus On Financial Freedom

"The key to financial freedom and great wealth is a person's ability or skill to convert earned income into passive income and/or portfolio income."
— Robert Kiyosaki

So, how do you start establishing passive income? In basic terms, the secret is to keep more money than you spend. Then, you use that money to make you more money, harnessing the power of compounding interest to create sustainable wealth.

It sounds relatively simple, right? However, in order to do this, you need to fight lifestyle inflation. When you were (maybe you still are) a broke 20-something, you probably lived on a small budget. But as you start earning more money, most people allow their spending to creep, buying a nicer house, nicer cars and more expensive clothes. You have a bigger paycheck, but not more money left over at the end of the month. Just more 'stuff.'

Consider this: most people work in order to afford their lifestyle. The wealthy, however, work to create and *buy assets that pay them* in order to afford their lifestyles. It's a subtle difference, but it is the difference between retiring early and struggling to keep up.

Here are the most common passive income streams that -- with a bit of time and effort -- can make your money work for you:

1. Interest -- Money paid on funds that you loan out (even to your bank).
2. Dividends -- Money that companies pay to stock shareholders.
3. Capital Gains -- Profits from the sale of property or investment.
4. Royalties -- Money paid for the use of intellectual property, like a patent or manuscript.
5. Rental Income -- Funds paid to you from a property you own.
6. Business Income -- Funds paid to you as the owner of a business.

You may have heard that millionaires average seven streams of passive income. Seven is not a magic number that will turn you into a millionaire. However, this saying highlights an important point: the wealthy understand the importance of having multiple sources of income.

Let's break down the passive income streams I'm working on building. I'm in the fortunate position to have additional cash from my day job to jump start my goal of financial freedom. I'm also a busy parent of two young boys so I'm trying to simplify the process as much as possible.

Investment Portfolio

Like the other 43 million households that own an individual retirement account, I have been contributing to my Roth 401k since my early twenties. As of February 2019, I have $406,690.58 (fully vested) in my retirement portfolio.

My investment strategy? Do what the best ever recommends. Warren Buffett recommends that most people (including his wife) should invest 90 percent of their money into a low cost stock index fund (S&P 500) and 10 percent into high quality short term municipal bonds. If it's good enough for Mrs. Buffett, it's good enough for me.

Buffett is so confident in this approach that he made a 10 year bet that an index fund (a portfolio that matches the makeup of the market) would outperform actively managed hedge funds (portfolios where experts pick stocks they think will perform well). He famously won that bet in 2017 and donated his money to charity. Not only did he win that bet -- he won by a large margin. His pick, the S&P 500, gained 125.8% over ten years. The actively-managed hedge funds averaged about 36 percent.

Buffett's philosophy is to ignore the "noise" about the stock market and to stick to big, easy decisions. This makes it easy to invest.

Yet, these simple investments can pay off big. Through the power of compounding, I estimate that I will accumulate $2.7 million in 18 years, if I continue to max out my retirement contribution at 18 percent, and average 9 percent growth rate (the average S&P rate of return since its inception 90 years ago). In this case, it pays to be average.

Real Estate Investment

I was inspired to get into the real estate investment game because so many people have accumulated wealth through it. After doing some research, my wife and I bought a two bedroom garden style condo, in an up-and-coming city with shops, restaurants and easy access to public transportation.

I had high hopes, but six months later and we're evicting our first ever tenant. I'm not sure the aggravation of dealing with bad tenants is worth the reward, based on our recent experience, but we're willing to give it another try.

This time, we'll be hiring a property manager to handle the day-to-day upkeep and finding qualified tenants. Property management companies generally charge 10 percent of rent. We won't be earning positive cash flow charging market rate rent, but we won't be losing money either. If rent increases (nominally) over time we'll eventually start earning positive cash flow while taking advantage of renters paying down the mortgage (earning equity over time) and tax benefits.

With any investment it's important to spread out your risk, but this is not possible when renting out a single unit. You're putting all your cash flow eggs into one tenant. However, you can hedge your bets in the real estate investment game by buying a multi-family or unit property, using real estate investment trusts, investing in commercial real estate, or participating in real estate crowdfunding. This will be my strategy for buying future real estate investments.

Layupforlife Blog and Social Media Property

Even though I'm new to blogging and digital marketing, I feel like I've learned and achieved a lot in the eight months I've been doing it. It's taken a lot of trying and failing, but I'm starting to find my groove.

I'm averaging 60-70 visitors every day on https://layupforlife.com, have passed the 12,000 mark for followers on Instagram, and am growing an email list. These are all assets that I own and will continue to improve. I've earned a couple hundred bucks in affiliate commissions, but will need to scale up by providing content that people want and respond to. I also plan on leveraging my online presence to promote e-books, courses and affiliate products.

Blogging and building a social media presence is a lot of upfront work and is not the most passive way to make income, but you can do it on your schedule. This is something I work on after the kids go to bed when I have a couple hours to myself. And, once it's rolling, it will provide a more passive income stream.

Dividend Stocks

A dividend is a share of the company's profits distributed to shareholders, usually quarterly. It is the company's way of thanking you, with a bonus, for owning shares in the company.

My strategy is to own a portfolio of dividend growth stocks that have growth potential and a consistent history of paying dividends. I balance in some blue chip (high quality) dividend stocks in four categories to diversify my risk:

1. Healthcare and pharmaceutical
2. Food and beverage (non-cyclical -- i.e, not affected by the overall economy)
3. Consumable basic needs (non-cyclical)
4. Industrials

These industries have been around for a long time and won't be going anywhere soon. Since dividends are generally paid by companies who are stable and have good cash flow, these industries are good bets on getting dividends.

A Note On Compound Interest

Dividend investing is also a great way to earn compound interest by taking part in a Dividend Re-Investment Plan or

DRIP. This is when you use the dividend payments to buy more shares of stock. Compound Interest is a simple yet powerful concept of reinvesting interest into the original principal sum; simply put, it's making interest on interest.

Consider this example from David Reiss, professor of law at Brooklyn Law School, who says:

"Would you rather receive a gift on Jan. 1 of $1 million, or a penny that doubles every day for the rest of the month? Most kids would go for the million bucks, but those who are patient enough to do the math know that they can get millions more if they are patient enough to wait the month."

It's true. The penny-doubler would finish January with $9.7 million more than his instant gratification-seeking friend.

I'm realistic and understand that you're not going to be doubling your money everyday; but if you earn a 10 percent return (the S&P 500 average historical return), minus fees, on your principal sum and reinvest those earnings and dividends, you will double your original amount in approximately 7.2 years.

I came up with this number by using the rule of 72, a formula used to estimate the number of years required to double invested money at a given annual rate of return.

Compound interest is more powerful when you add, to your original principal sum, each year.

My plan is to invest $20,000 initially and $20,000 each year thereafter. At a 10 percent annual return, my compound interest calculator calculates that my future value in 5 years will be $166,522.40. At 10 years, my future value will be $402,498.19. After 22 years -- when my kids should be out of college -- my value will be $1,733,665.99, all from a $20,000 investment.

Here is the breakdown of profits by year:

- 5 years at 10% return - $166,522.40 (total sum with earnings) - $100,000 (principal sum) = $66,522.40 (total profit)

- 10 years at 10% return - $402,498.19 (total sum with earnings) - $200,000 (principal sum) = $202,498.19 (total profit)
- 22 years at 10% return - $1,733,665.99 (total sum with earnings) - $440,000 (principal sum) = $1,293,665.99 (total profit)

I'll be ecstatic if my returns are close to these estimates and I plan on getting there with Dividend Growth Stock Investing.

Looking 22 years down the road, my passive income (if I choose to take cash dividend distributions) can be estimated at 4 percent of $1,733,665.99, or $69,346.64 per year

At that point in my life, I hope to be close to done paying my mortgage and paying for my kids' secondary education, so nearly $70,000 in a decent sum of money. This is in addition to what I will have in my 401k, which gives me a lot of financial flexibility. I can keep reinvesting the dividends or live off of them.

Other streams of passive income.

In addition to the passive income streams I'm already building, I have plans to expand into more in the future. Here's what I'm looking at

- **E-books**

  This is my first e-book and I plan on writing many more. The beauty of this asset is that I hope to continue to make money off of it long after I publish it. Granted, it is a ton of upfront work and hours invested, and a gamble, because I might not sell copies. The way I see it, it's a passion project and I have nothing to lose whether it sells or not.

My strategy is to carefully research the correct niche in Kindle Direct Publishing to place it under. The trick is to find the perfect balance of enough demand versus category saturation. The benefit of publishing through Kindle is the built-in market. The key is to write compelling content that readers respond to, in order to rank high in your sub-category. SEO and keyword research is helpful when launching your book, since these will help you rank higher in Google search.

In addition to using Kindle, I will leverage my social media audience of 10,000 people, as well as using other influencers to promote my ebook. I will also sell the book directly on my website.

- **Online courses**

After I publish a book that enough people respond positively to, I plan on expanding that information into online e-courses. E-courses are another learning method for people to use. These courses are particularly useful for people with learning differences (like my ADD) because they can take their time reviewing the course.

E-courses allow students to learn through a combination of: video, learning slides, quizzes and games. Developing this asset will take a lot of upfront work, but I will then be able to money off of it long after I finish developing your online course.

- **Coworking spaces**

Our modern gig economy has made the freelance community explode and has allowed anyone to create an online business. Thousands of people now work full-time as freelancers or remote workers. While working from home has benefits, many of these people find they want a physical space outside their homes where they can work.

Compared to coffee shops, co-working spaces offer quieter environments to concentrate in, private conference rooms to hold meetings in, a public space to host events, and fast and reliable internet?

Companies like Wework have capitalized on co-working spaces, but there are still underserved markets. I have a couple of ideas that I need to research and flesh out further. This business is a higher risk because of the upfront capital I would need need to bring to the table, but is a great mix of online and traditional brick and mortar business with potentially big payoffs.

9

TOP TEN TAKEAWAYS

Getting your shit together is no small task. I've presented a lot of information in this book, but you shouldn't feel overwhelmed. Here are the top ten steps for success:

1. Own your shit.

The first critical step in getting your shit together is self reflection and owning your shit. Are you happy? Are you where you want to be in life? How do you want your life to look?

Hold yourself responsible for the status of your life. Whatever you want to achieve in life must start with understanding your reality and taking responsible for changing it.

2. Cultivate conscientiousness.

The single biggest personality trait successful people have in common is conscientiousness -- a drive to do your duties thoroughly. Conscientiousness has been linked with higher salaries, better ability to hold a job and more job satisfaction. People who measure as highly conscientious have higher test scores, less disease and more success. That's what we all want, right?

Conscientiousness is a trait that can be practiced and developed over time through repetition, so focus on building this quality. Start by keeping tidy, setting a schedule and practicing mindfulness. All of this will help you get your shit together.

3. Make mental health a priority.

Mental health is important for your success and achieving your goals. One in 5 American adults have a mental illness and it is estimated that mental illness causes $193.2 billion in lost earnings every year. No one wants to talk about mental illness because it is still stigmatized, but mental health is critical for you to lead a stable and fulfilling life.

Eating well, exercising and being mindful all support good mental health. So does time off. And when you need it, don't be afraid to reach out for professional help.

4. Form your 'team' and get the help you need.

Let other people help you along your path. Cultivate meaningful relationships. Seek professional health support and fellowship if you need it. Find a mentor.

Remember, nobody achieves anything in life alone. There is no weakness in relying on others for support. Sometimes you need a team to get your shit together. Just remember to give back at least as much as you take.

5. Take self care seriously.

You need to make sure you're taking care of yourself. It's not good for anybody if you're overworked, stressed or tired. Eat well, work out and get plenty of sleep. This will help you feel better and perform better professionally.

Remember to step away. Taking time to take care for yourself will allow you to be more productive. You'll also make better decisions because your brain won't be under duress.

6. Plan for the future.

If you're trying to get your shit together, you're probably already working toward something. Keep that momentum going by setting manageable and specific goals. Set deadlines and hold yourself accountable. Have mini-goals along the way to reaching your long-term goals, and remember to re-evaluate your path every now and then to make sure your goals align with your priorities and values.

7. Educate yourself.

In order to achieve your goals, you need to learn skills that will help you execute actions along the way. For some people this means studying in school, while others it means apprenticeships or other trainings. For all people, building "soft skills" like emotional intelligence and communication are critical.

Remember that an education is never complete. Always challenge yourself to grow, and make an effort to continue your learning through podcasts, online courses and other material.

8. Surround yourself with the right people.

You won't get your shit together if you are surrounded by people who are living in chaos. Take an honest look at your life and the people you spend the most time with. Think about who is a positive influence and who brings you down with their negativity and drama.

A critical step is to surround yourself with people who have the same goals as you. Don't waste your resources on people who take your time and energy without giving anything back. These people will drain you until you have nothing left if you let them. Let go of people and relationships that bring you down.

9. Maximize your earned income, budget and save.

Maximize your earned income by knowing what you're good at, learning how to market yourself, and asking for what you're worth. Continue to cultivate skills to make you the best at what you do. Your reputation will travel and bring you more work. Negotiate your salary and raises when you're hired and during performance reviews.

Learn to budget your money and cut down on unnecessary expenses. Remember that every dollar that is invested or used to pay down debt will bring you even more money in return.

10. Put your money to work.

There are only so many hours in a day and so many days of the week that you can work. That means there's a natural cap on your earned income potential. That's why you need to put your money to work for you.

The wealthy learn to make money passively through multiple income streams. That's how you build sustainable wealth. Pay down debt, maximize your retirement contributions, consider real estate investments, and work toward building assets that pay you back.

EPILOGUE

Money Isn't Everything

When you picked this book up, you made the conscious decision to do something about your lot in life. You made the decision to better yourself; to get your shit together. Give yourself credit for that.

We've focused a lot on making more money. After all, nothing in life is free. You need money to live, eat, and sleep. You want travel the world? Want to spend your life doing charitable work? It costs money to do so.

Yet, studies show that once you earn enough money to cover your basic necessities and have a little extra for vacation, your level of happiness tapers off. That's because money isn't everything. No matter how rich you are, you're still human and live on earth. You're still mortal and bleed like everyone else. You still go through emotional ups and downs just like the rest of us.

The point of this book is to help guide you to get your shit together and make money. But you also need to understand that money is the means to an end. Money and passive income will buy you time and the freedom to live the way you want.

What will you do with your freedom?

I am still figuring that out myself. My five-year plan is to have enough cash on hand to support my family's needs and have the freedom to do anything with my career. As much as I love my job and career, I want to have the confidence and freedom to pursue new opportunities in life.

This leaves me with options. I would never recommend that you quit your job to pursue a new venture. If you want to start a business, do it from a position of power. Set yourself up so that if your business venture doesn't work out, you have something to fall back on. Be confident and stay loose. That's when we make our best decisions. You can't be uptight or all-in because then you make decisions based out of fear.

As you think about your five-year plan and your long-term goals, remember that money isn't everything. Having your shit together doesn't necessarily mean making more money. It means being in a position where you have options. That means you can pursue whatever speaks to you. And who wouldn't want that option?

22437368R00047

Printed in Great Britain
by Amazon